Contents

Words in **bold** are explained in the glossary on page 30.

What are flowering plants?

Flowering plants are plants that produce flowers.

There are many, many different types of

flowering plants.

Roses have beautiful flowers made up of lots of petals. Many roses also have a sweet smell.

Many trees, such as this flowering cherry, produce flowers.

Flowers grow in a wonderful range of colours and shapes. They are produced at certain times of the year. Without flowers, plants could not produce their fruits and **seeds**.

Flowering plants such as grasses, daisies and poppies can be found in meadows.

5

Inside a flower

Most flowers have petals which may be brightly coloured. Sometimes, the petals are joined together to form a tube shape.

The male part of a flower is called the **stamen**. This is made up of an **anther** on a stalk. The anther releases a powdery yellow dust called **pollen**.

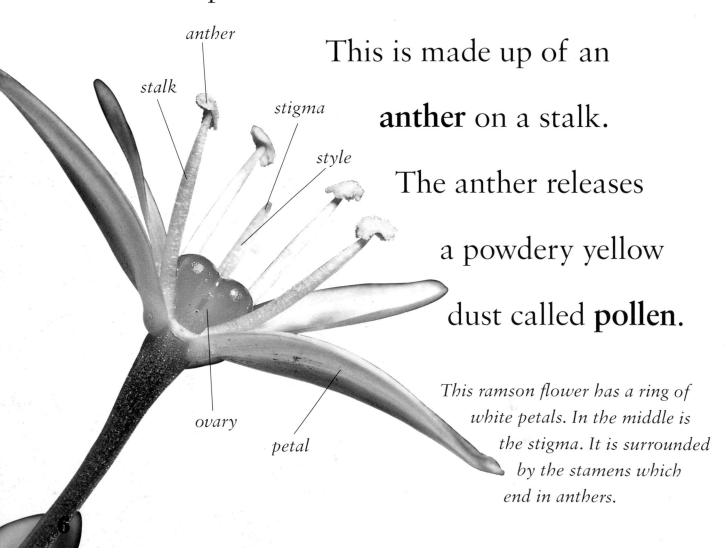

anther

stalk

stigma

style

ovary

petal

This ramson flower has a ring of white petals. In the middle is the stigma. It is surrounded by the stamens which end in anthers.

The anthers and stigma of the hibiscus flower are found on a long stalk that sticks out above the petals.

The female part is called the **carpel**.

This is made up of a **stigma**, which is joined to the **ovary** by a stalk called the **style**. Most flowers have both anthers and carpels, but a few have separate **male and female flowers**.

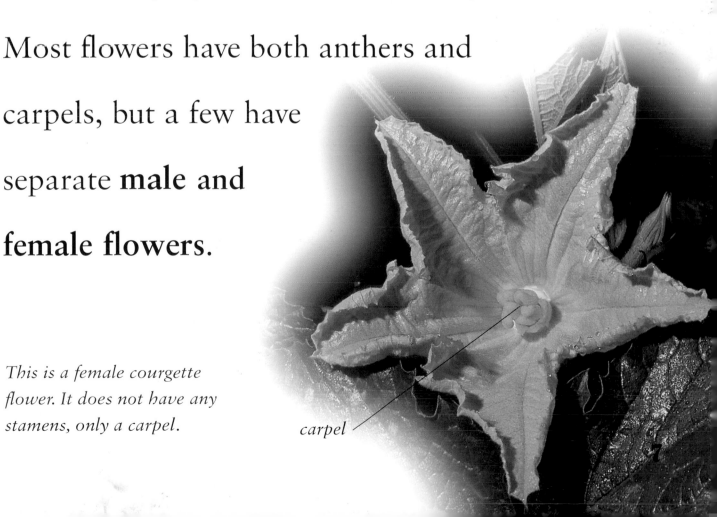

carpel

This is a female courgette flower. It does not have any stamens, only a carpel.

All types of flowers

Flowers can be small or large, colourful or plain. Some flowers are grouped together to form **flower spikes** and clusters.

The flower of the sunflower can be huge. It has a ring of yellow petals, which surround a ring of anthers. In the middle there is a mass of carpels.

The red hot poker produces a flower spike. The flowers open at the bottom first. By the time the flowers at the top of the spike have opened, the ones near the bottom are dying.

The flowers of the grass plant don't look like flowers at all. They are small and green. The long anthers hang outside the flower and they release lots of pollen. Some trees, such as

The yellow flower of the sunflower grows at the top of the stem of the plant.

the willow and hazel, produce separate male and female flowers. The male flower is called a catkin.

Millions of tiny pollen grains drop from a catkin when it is moved in the wind.

Pollination

To make a seed, pollen has to be moved from the anthers of one flower to the stigma of another. This is called pollination. The pollen may be carried by animals such as bees, bats and birds, or carried in the wind or by water.

The bright red petals of the tulip attract insects into the middle of the flower.

Hummingbirds visit flowers to sip the sugary nectar. As they push their heads deep into the flowers their feathers pick up pollen from the anthers.

Flowers have many ways of attracting animals, such as large, brightly coloured petals. They may also produce sweet smells and **nectar,** which is a sugary liquid that animals like to drink as a food.

This bee has become covered in pollen as it crawls over the sunflower in search of nectar.

Unusual flowers

Some plants need flies to **pollinate** their flowers. They attract the flies by producing a smell that is like rotting meat. Flies crawl all over the flower in search of the meat and they become covered in pollen.

The huge flower of the Rafflesia plant smells of rotting meat. It grows on the ground of rainforests. Flies pick up pollen as they crawl inside.

The flower of the bird of paradise has a landing platform for birds. As the birds land, the stamens rub pollen onto their feet.

Other flowers have odd shapes to make sure that animals become covered in pollen when they visit the flower. As an insect crawls through a flower, pollen may be dropped onto its back. Sometimes insects have to squeeze through tiny gaps to reach the nectar and they become covered in pollen.

These visiting bees have to crawl right inside the tube-shaped flower of the foxglove to reach the nectar.

Orchids

Orchids are a group of plants

This orchid is growing on rocks in a rainforest.

that have some amazing flowers.

They grow around the world, on grasslands, on

mountain sides and in forests. Some of the most

beautiful orchids are found in rainforests.

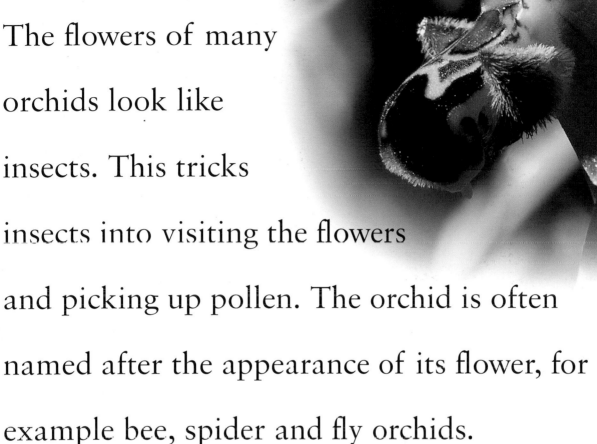

The petals at the centre of this bee orchid look just like a large bumble bee.

The flowers of many orchids look like insects. This tricks insects into visiting the flowers and picking up pollen. The orchid is often named after the appearance of its flower, for example bee, spider and fly orchids.

This very strange orchid looks like a small insect.

What is a fruit?

A plant can make its seeds once its flower has been pollinated. First, the petals **wither** and drop off. Then the **ovary** swells and starts to change into a fruit. The seeds grow inside the fruit. The job of the fruit is to protect the seeds until they are ready to be released.

Each of these red berries has been formed from an ovary. The remains of the flower can be seen at the bottom of the spike.

The red flesh of the tomato is the fruit. The seeds are found inside the tomato.

Some fruits contain a single seed, such as plums and cherries. But other fruits, such as tomatoes and rosehips, contain lots of seeds.

Nuts are fruits. The hard outer covering is the fruit. This forms a case to protect the seed which is inside.

Nuts contain a single large seed which many animals like to eat. Animals such as squirrels bite through the hard outside case of the nut to reach the seed inside.

Colourful fruits

Fruits come in many colours, shapes and sizes. They include plums, apples and oranges, berries and nuts. Many fruits are sweet and good to eat. Others are hard and dry. The fruits of the pepper plant are very colourful – they can be red, green, orange or yellow.

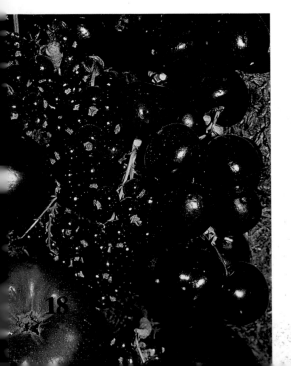

Redcurrants, plums and cherries are an attractive red colour. They are sweet tasting and can be eaten raw or cooked.

How many different types of fruits can you spot in this photograph?

Citrus fruits such as oranges and lemons have a thick skin, or peel, which has a bitter taste. Inside the fruits are divided into small parts called segments. One of the largest fruits is the pumpkin. A ripe pumpkin can weigh many kilograms.

Brightly coloured pumpkins are picked in autumn. Many pumkins are used as decorations for Hallowe'en.

Animals and fruits

Many animals like to eat fruits because they taste sweet. In autumn, the fruits of many road-side plants such as blackberries and rosehips are eaten by birds and small mammals such as voles and mice.

A bank vole clambers over this plant to reach the red fruits.

Rainforest fruits

are eaten by fruit bats,

monkeys and birds such

as toucans and macaws.

The fruits are swallowed and digested (or

broken down) in the animal's

gut. But many seeds pass

through the gut without

being harmed. They pass

out of the animal's body in

its droppings.

This yellow and blue macaw holds a fruit in its claw. It uses its large beak to break it into smaller pieces.

Seeds

Birds like to eat sunflower seeds as part of their food.

Seeds form inside a fruit. A seed has a tough outer covering called a seed coat. This protects the seed. Inside the seed there is a tiny **embryo** that will become a new plant. There is also a store of food. The food will be used by the young plant once it starts to grow.

Maize is an important food plant. The yellow seeds grow on a cob. The type of maize called sweetcorn produces seeds which are sweet to eat.

Some seeds are swollen with food. For this reason they are important foods, for example peas, beans and lentils. The seeds of **cereal plants** are also important foods. Cereal plants include wheat, rice and maize. These seeds are used in our food every day.

The Coco de Mer palm tree produces a fruit that weighs up to 30 kilograms (shown below). Inside is a single seed. This is the largest seed produced by any plant.

Spreading seeds

Seeds can be spread by the wind, by water and by animals. Some fruits and seeds hitch a ride on an animal. The **burr** for example, has a prickly covering that is caught up in the fur of passing animals.

Hundreds of seeds are carefully packed into the pod of the milkweed. Each seed has a parachute of fluffy white threads that float on the wind.

Coconuts can float and they drift in the water until they are washed up on beaches.

Some seeds are spread by the wind. These seeds are light and some have their own mini **parachutes** which carry them away when the wind blows. Some seeds have wings, such as the maple and sycamore. The wings keep the seed in the air for longer so the seed travels further.

This Shetland pony has picked up lots of burrs in its shaggy coat.

Growing seeds

A plant begins life when the seed starts to **germinate** or grow. The seed takes in water and swells up. Then the outer seed coat splits. Inside, the tiny plant starts to grow, using the food stored inside the seed.

seed

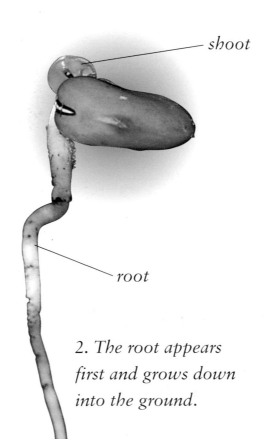

shoot

root

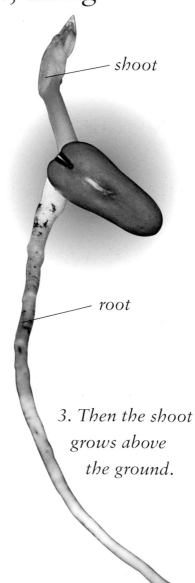

shoot

root

1. The seed swells with water and the seed coat splits.

2. The root appears first and grows down into the ground.

3. Then the shoot grows above the ground.

Soon after it rains in the desert, many seeds germinate. This desert is covered in a mass of Californian poppies.

Seeds need the right conditions to germinate. All seeds need water, but some need a lot of warmth or light. A few will only grow after a fire or after they have experienced freezing temperatures.

Many tree seeds germinate in spring. They quickly produce new leaves before they are shaded by the leaves of larger trees.

Investigate!

Growing flowers

Insects have their favourite types of flowers. Hoverflies and brightly coloured flower beetles like to visit open flowers. They crawl over the surface of the flower and pick up pollen. Moths and butterflies have long tongues so they can reach deep into tube-shaped flowers. Try growing your own plants from seed. Seeds of plants such as marigolds, Californian poppies and sunflowers grow very quickly. If you sow the seeds in spring, you will get flowers by summer. You can buy packets of seed in many shops.

Bees are attracted to marigolds.

What to do:

• Take an old margarine tub and punch some holes in the bottom. Fill it with **potting compost.**

• Water the compost well before you sow your seeds. If you have very small seeds sprinkle them over the top of the compost and then cover them with a thin layer of compost. Sunflower seeds are larger and can be pushed into the compost.

• Place the tub on a sunny window ledge.

• Check it every day and water the soil if necessary.

The seedlings will appear after a week or so.
• Once they have grown a few leaves they should be replanted in a larger pot.
• Your plants can be planted outside in early summer.

Looking closely at fruits

Always ask an adult for help when using sharp objects such as knives.

Don't forget to water your plants regularly.

Carefully cut your fruits in half.

Fruits are very varied inside. Fruits such as oranges and tomatoes are made up of lots of smaller segments. An apple has a fleshy part that surrounds the middle or core. The core is made up of segments and these contain seeds.

What to do:

• Carefully cut some different fruits in half. How many seeds can you see?

A bean has a pod that you can open up to reveal the seeds. The largest seeds are usually found at one end of the pod. A courgette or marrow is made up of a fleshy white pulp and the seeds are found towards the middle.

Glossary

anther The male part of the flower which produces the pollen.

burr A prickly seed that sticks to the fur of animals and to clothing.

carpel The name given to the female parts of the flower.

cereal plants Grasses that have seeds which can be eaten. Wheat, rice and maize are cereals.

embryo The young, tiny plant that grows within a seed.

flower spikes Flowers that are made up of many smaller flowers attached to a long stem. The flower of the foxglove plant is a flower spike.

germinate To grow from a seed into a seedling.

gut A long tube running through the body in which food is broken down and taken into the body.

male and female flowers A male flower has stamens and no carpels. A female flower has carpels but no stamens.

nectar The sugary liquid produced by plants to attract insects and other animals.

ovary The part of the flower where the seeds form.

parachutes Umbrella-shaped attachments that slow down the speed at which objects fall to the ground.

pollen Tiny yellow grains that look like dust.

pollinate To transfer pollen from the anther of one flower to the stigma of another.

potting compost Soil that has been treated so that it is suitable for growing plants from seeds.

ripe Fruits or seeds that are fully grown and ready to be eaten.

seeds The grains or nuts from which new plants may grow.

stamen The name given to the male parts of a flower.

stigma The part of the flower which receives the pollen.

style The part of the flower that joins the stigma to the ovary.

wither To become dry and then die.

31

Index